OUTHOUSE
HUMOR

OUTHOUSE HUMOR

HUMOR
BILLY EDD WHEELER

By the composer of the hit song "Ode to the Little Brown Shack Out Back"

A collection of jokes,
stories, songs, and
poems about outhouses
and thundermugs,
corncobs and honey-
dippers, wasps and
spiders and Sears
and Roebuck catalogues

Illustrations by Wendell E. Hall

August House / Little Rock
P U B L I S H E R S

Published by August House, Inc.,
P.O. Box 3223, Little Rock, Arkansas, 72203,
501-663-7300.

Printed in the United States of America

10 9 8 7 6 5 4

LIBRARY OF CONGRESS CATALOGING-IN-PUBLICATION DATA
Wheeler, Billy Edd.
Outhouse humor: a collection of jokes, stories, songs,
and poems about outhouses and thundermugs,
corncobs and honey-dippers, wasps and spiders,
and Sears and Roebuck catalogues / Billy Edd Wheeler.
p. cm.
ISBN 0-87483-058-3 (pkb.: alk. paper)
1. Outhouses — Anecdotes, facetiae, satire, etc.
2. American wit and humor. I. Title.
PN6231.097W47 1988
817'.54'080355 — dc19
87-31666
CIP

Cover illustration by Wendell E. Hall
Illustrations by Wendell E. Hall and Boyd Carr
Production artwork by Ira Hocut
Typography by Diversified Graphics, Little Rock, AR
Design direction by Ted Parkhurst
Project direction by Hope Coulter

"Mama Was Blue in the Face" and "Of Outhouses and Cherry Trees"
were previously published in *Laughter in Appalachia* (August House,
1987) and are used by permission.

This book is printed on archival-quality paper which meets the
guidelines for performance and durability of the Committee on
Production Guidelines for Book Longevity of the Council on Library
Resources.

AUGUST HOUSE, INC.   PUBLISHERS   LITTLE ROCK

To all those hardy souls all over America, living and dead, whose feet trod the paths to the little shacks out back...in appreciation of shared memories, trials and tribulations, dreams, and laughter...especially laughter.

Acknowledgments

Thanks to Jim Comstock and his faithful readers of the *West Virginia Hillbilly* for all their contributions, listed individually under their material in the book, and to those whose material was not used.

To Rose Mary Evans for help with research on the outhouses of England, and to her parents, Wilson and Ellen Evans, for getting us in touch.

To Ray Stevens, the genius of country music, for loaning me his book and telling me some tales. And to his buddy and mine, Chet Atkins, C.G.P. (Certified Guitar Picker), for his help and support of the project.

To George Brosi and Loyal Jones for help with research and actual story contributions.

To Boyd Carr, for drawings and 4 answering the call 4 lore.

To Mary Wheeler for helpful suggestions in formatting and dedicating the book.

Contents

© boyd carr 1979

1

Spotlighting the Lowly Outhouse

Don't let 'em tear that little brown building down
For there's not another like it
In the country or the town—

I wrote that chorus several years ago when I was living in
New York City, trying to get started as a songwriter. The
song it's from, "Ode to the Little Brown Shack Out Back,"
was suggested to me by two sources. One was the *West Virginia Hillbilly,* a newspaper published 'weakly' by that
great West Virginian Jim Comstock, a journalist-philosopher-humorist all rolled into one.

Jim wrote most of the paper himself under his headings
"The Comstock Load" and "Editor on the Go." But he featured poems now and then on a page he called "Old Likker
in a New Jug," and it was there I first read the James Whitcomb Riley poem "The Passing of the Backhouse." (This
poem is included in the chapter "The Muses Visit the
Outhouse" and was the inspiration for a later song, "Ode

To Granny And The Little Brown Shack Out Back," also included.) From time to time Jim would make mention of Chic Sales, another man who had written about outhouses.

But it never dawned on me to write a song about an outhouse until my good friend Judy Stammer (she was Judy Drukker then, a goodwill ambassador and fund-raiser for Berea College under President Francis S. Hutchins) told me about some town's passing an ordinance against outhouses, saying that if you had an outhouse within the city limits you'd have to tear it down. I think it was a Kentucky town right across the river from Cincinnati. Covington, maybe.

I laughed about it, said in mock seriousness, "Now, wouldn't it be a shame if all the outhouses all over America were torn down? It would be a catastrophe. A national landmark would disappear forever. Judy, we can't let this happen!"

"Well, then, you'll have to write a song about it."

So I did.

There's Gold in Them-There Outhouses

It was a protest song. This was in the sixties when songwriters were protesting everything that moved. I was living in New York City, so I was caught up in it too. Phil Ochs, Pete Seeger, and my buddy Tom Paxton were protesting against war and hate and pollution and Bob Dylan was getting in his licks too, even writing a protest song against boxing ("Who Killed Davey Moore") and I wrote my share, especially against things like strip mining. Judy Collins recorded three of them, "The Coming of the Roads," "Red-Winged Black Bird," and "Coal Tattoo," which was also recorded by The Kingston Trio about the time they recorded my first really big hit, "The Reverend Mr. Black."

But "Ode to the Little Brown Shack Out Back" was not serious. It was a tongue-in-cheek protest, written by a very poor country boy living in a concrete jungle, yearning to be where there were hills and trees and grass, trout streams and swimming holes, country stores and kinfolks. I needed a good laugh.

So I wrote the song and took it to the president of my record label, Dave Kapp of Kapp Records, and he turned it down, turned up his nose and said in his most distinguished, sophisticated voice: "No, Billy Edd. We want to get you a hit record, but we don't have to do it with you singing songs about outdoor toilets!"

I first sang "Ode to the Little Brown Shack Out Back" at the Mountain State Arts and Crafts Fair in Ripley, West Virginia. Jim Comstock was on the program, too, so while we waited to be introduced I asked him to look over my new song. I said, "My wife Mary thinks it's too risqué. What do you think?"

Here's how he reported the incident in the *Hillbilly* on August 27, 1987:

> I gave it a hasty reading, and then went over it again. I loved it. And told him that was the best thing he had done so far. "The audience will love it," I whispered. And indeed they did when it was Billy Edd's time to go on. They applauded and demanded he sing it again. Later, at the luncheon which followed, he was asked to sing it again. If I had been just slightly fuddy-duddy and told him it was too off-color, I actually believe he would have attic-ed it and thus would the world have lost one of its merriest songs.

I am amazed at Jim's memory. My own memory shows me a picture of him roaring with laughter and wanting a copy of the lyrics, which I had written down on the back of a shoebox, to print in his newspaper. That was over twenty years ago. A lot of water has run under the privy since then. Jim has sold his newspaper, gotten old enough to qualify for his annual Past-Eighty parties, founded a University of Hard Knocks, survived a heart attack and open heart surgery, bought his newspaper back when it almost died, and is still going strong.

Well, people wanted to buy "Ode to the Little Brown Shack Out Back" there at the fair and, really, everywhere I sang it. So when a fellow from Paducah, Kentucky, recorded it live while I was singing at a "hootenanny," I got a copy of it from him, just me and my guitar and the laughter of the crowd, and sent it to New York.

"If you don't want to release it," I wrote Mr. Kapp, "then please give me a waiver, or something, and I'll spend my own money and have it pressed myself. From the reaction I'm getting, I know I can sell it."

Mr. Kapp wired me right back. He'd had a change of heart. He wrote, "We like it...We're releasing it immediately."

"Outhouse-mania" Sweeps the Country

So "The Shack" was released. A few disc jockeys played it, but it was banned in Boston (really), Washington, and several other places, and maybe that helped it. It made Billboard's Hot 100. Of course, it was not dirty or suggestive—it's a nursery rhyme compared to today's fare—but we're talking over twenty years ago. But it did get on the charts, so I had a record. I was a budding star! I started doing country music package shows with people like Loretta Lynn, Sonny James, George Hamilton IV, Pete Drake (the great steel guitarist), David Houston, Tommy Cash (Johnny's brother), and others, plus some college concerts and county fairs.

I played Sarasota, where it was a hit. The owner of the

radio station told me, "I was afraid to play it because I'd heard it was off-color, but I went up to the DJ Convention in Nashville a few weeks ago and when I got within fifty miles of the city I heard Ralph Emery play it on WSM. So I pulled off the road, called back down here and told my jocks, 'Open her up!' And, by golly, it was a hit by the time I got back."

The song still didn't make it big. It simmered on the charts for about six months. Then a big Atlanta pop station started playing it as a novelty, and it sold 25,000 records in a week. It hit in Norfolk, Virginia, and of course West Virginia stations were playing it, and some other stations from Maine to California, so it got a "bullet" in Billboard and went to #2, and I had me a hit.

A DJ in Nashville sent me a clipping from a Nashville newspaper showing his station's weekly charts. "The Shack" was #1, with the Beatles at #2, #5, and #9. The Beatles were hot. But for one week, one week, that lowly edifice featuring the once most popular seat in the nation was hotter.

I say *it* was hotter because it was the song and not me that was selling. The public bought the song, not the artist. My star faded. Oh, I had other chart records, and I released a lot of albums. I had a shot. I sang at The Grand Old Opry and the Newport Folk Festival, at Carnegie Hall and goat ropin's, colleges and coffeehouses, in country music lounges (skull orchards, they call them in the trade) and on syndicated TV shows. But I never became a big recording artist.

My Cup Runneth Over with Outhouses

What I did become was an expert on outhouses, and I became a collector of outhouse lore without even trying. People sent me poems and songs and stories about

15

outhouses, paintings and pictures and carvings of outhouses, and once when I was singing at a mall in Pittsburgh a lady rushed to the stage and presented me with a salt-and-pepper shaker set in the form of tiny outhouses. I never used them. For some reason I just couldn't sprinkle anything on my food that came out of an outhouse.

But I thanked the lady. And to make conversation apropos of her gift I said, "You know, my granddaddy lives in Dogpatch, West Virginia, and he has an outhouse in his back yard. When I go see him, about once a year, I use his outhouse."

"Oh, buddy," she exclaimed, "it's every day with us. Every day!"

It was satisfying to me to see how my song touched so many people, many of them people who bought my record because they now lived in the city and this was a pleasant reminder of home, back home in the country. Some of them bought records at county fairs to send to relatives and friends who had moved away. They bought them four and five at a time.

Precious Memories of Outhouses

I was a teenager before I experienced the gurgling wonder and convenience of indoor toilets. I loved them. But it's nice to remember the old days, too, to stroll down memory lane in my mind to that time when I ate my grandmother's cornbread and beans, homemade buttermilk and sauerkraut cooked with short ribs, to the fodder shocks and frost on the pumpkin, to hellfire-and-damnation preachers, kissing the girls while playing "post office" or "spin-the-bottle," and rooting the match stick out of the ground with my nose, chin, and teeth after losing a jack-knife game of "root-the-peg" (some called it "root-hog-or-die"). Memories are precious. And as much as I hated going to the bathroom in the outhouse in the icy cold of winter, making the visit as brief as possible for fear of spiders and snakes (you've got to admit that it's a pretty precarious position to assume, with some of your most tender parts exposed to the elements and critters down there in the dark, especially if you've got a vivid imagination), it is still a cherished part of my memory.

Today outhouses are called Port-a-Johns or Johnnies-on-the-spot. You see them at construction jobs or outdoor concerts, sporting events or county fairs. They are made of plastic or fiberglass, these 'necessary rooms,' with the smooth round-edged look of modern, pre-molded mass production. But once they were the real thing with personalities to match their builders (and users), one-holers, two and three-holers, short, tall, stately or funny-looking, painted, unpainted, carpeted or bare. And, alas, now they have all but disappeared from the landscape.

"The times they are a-changing," the Bob Dylan song goes, and I have never been against change. But they can never tear the outhouses down in my mind.

Using the outhouse was kind of fun, actually. And when you got to go, you got to go, whether it's indoors or outdoors, in outer space or in a foxhole, up a tree or on the train. So you might as well laugh about it. That's what I've been doing ever since I had my one hit and people started telling me all these outhouse jokes.

A good laugh should be shared. So I gathered all the "got-to-go" stories I could find and put them into this book. Some of them are outrageous. Some are corny. Most are funny (I hope), whether you ever got to sit down and meditate in a real outhouse or not.

18

2

Outhouse Lore from the **West Virginia Hillbilly**

THOUGHTS FROM AN "EDITOR ON THE GO"

I would like to set the record straight. Outhouse lore is humorous now, simply because that example of early architecture is now all but passé, supplemented by a sanitary bathroom and plumbing. There was a time nobody laughed, and I am a survivor of that era. One of the strangest things in our civilization is that the three elements of body elimination—the body part that performs it, the act of doing it, and the place where it is done—are all no-no's in polite conversation. I know of no place in the Scriptures, in mythology, even history that the three are anything but moot points.

I was amused by William Safire's fumbling for a substitute for that little three-letter word for the rear of the human being, in his recent *New York Times* stint, stating that the national dread of the word "is expressed variously as *rear end, butt, behind, backside, tail, seat,* or if you are President Reagan, *keister."*

And the act itself is skirted likewise by all of us. Recently I heard that arch-feminist Sally Struthers tell on TV about an ideal convention she had attended where male and female adults "eliminated together, openly, without embarrassment." Lord, think of the other substitutes our language has for that nasty little four-letter word. In my family the word was "dump." My oldest brother's children when small referred to the two forms of elimination as "number one" and "number two." Women today are excused to "go to the powder room." Men depart a group to "write a check," or "see a man about a dog." Kids in school raise their hands.

Sir Thomas Crapper's Contribution

I was born and spent my early years in a frontier, backwoods lumbering town, where, while most of the homes had running water, the bathroom hadn't caught up. My family had an outdoors job which my mother referred to as the "closet," that word coming, of course, from "water closet," the gift to civilization of Sir Thomas Crapper, who was awarded a knighthood by Queen Victoria. This term was a bit strong for some Puritanical souls, who used "W.C." instead.

Honey-Dippers

The outhouse of my early Richwood days, the closet, I mean, escaped the services of the "honey-dippers" of that day and time, those sturdy souls who were sent periodically to remove the contents. I don't know whether the word is known elsewhere or not. I checked a number of dictionaries and found every kind of honey connection except dippers. Some years ago I got the idea of reprinting some ancient Town Council minutes and raised a not inconsiderable howl when it was recorded that the honey-dipper services of a certain businessman's father were required at the city hall privy.

Honey-dipping was always done at night, and I can recall my mother closing the door to keep the pungent aroma out, and always remarking that Cristys, or Straders, or whoever were cleaning their closets. I often wondered how she could so pinpoint the source of the odor.

We didn't avail ourselves of the services of honey-dippers and the cart they brought along, because we always used candy buckets, common objects back in that day which were available from any grocery store when your name came up to the top of the waiting list. The buckets were made of wood and had bales which facilitated their being snaked up from the depths when they reached the overflowing point. Also, my mother always kept a keg of lime handy to be scooped down the holes once or twice a week. Life back there was pretty challenging, and there was little to be merry about that little brown shack. Only it wasn't brown, but white, whitewashed by a Tom Sawyer called Jim, me. Inside and out.

(In England honey-dippers were called "rakers" or "gongfermors," and their honey wagons were called "lavender carts."—B.E.W.)

Don't Leave Home without It

When I got a job at the tannery the boss, in indoctrinating me, took me out along the river to show me the "necessary house" (William Byrd's name for his outhouse at Westover), a long open structure sitting over a stream of water which flowed into the Cherry River. I can still recall that first scene of some fifteen or twenty workers sitting in a long row answering the call of nature.

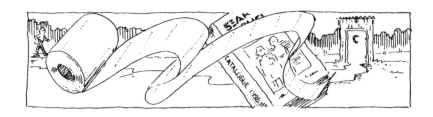

Later that day, after delaying the call as long as I could before my initial visit, I made my way there, waited for a user to leave, and then took his place. The man next to me was a huge giant of a man. He said, "New on the job, eh? Here, take this." He handed me a crumpled piece of paper. "Do it this way," he said. He showed me how to soften the paper by kneading it over and over in my hands. After that I knew the importance of having a supply of paper with me before going to work. I never left home without it.

One fellow, a farmer, kept a couple of corncobs as a paper substitute. I suppose there was toilet paper then, but I don't remember its being a must on my mother's grocery list. What else would one do with the Sears-Roebuck catalogue or the *Nicholas Republican?* On Hinkle Mountain on the farm, if we had to go, we "hit the bushes."

(In the north of England, folks used sycamore leaves, at least until autumn came. Those who could not afford a daily paper used rags. In one outhouse, or "lavatory," was this note on the wall:

If in this place
You find no paper
Behind the door
You'll find a scraper.

Caught out in the fields, instead of "hitting the bushes," people would find a ditch or a hedge and take a "country one," wiping with a handful of grass, hay, or straw. The Romans who settled England were a very clean race and washed themselves using sponges on sticks which were kept in containers of salt water or dipped into running water. Poorer Romans often used stone shells or herbs to clean themselves, but ladies favored goose feathers because they were soft.—B.E.W.)

A Roosevelt Bungalow

Somewhere among the maze of my collectibles is an early 1940 *Clarksburg Exponent* with a front-page streamer announcing that the country's fifty-thousandth Roosevelt bungalow would be dedicated that particular day. Few of the younger generation of today could conceive of President Roosevelt's desire to give rural Americans a new deal in their little shacks out back with crews of WPA laborers visiting farms and replacing their old dilapidated structures with spanking new ones. I'll never forget my father-in-law-to-be, Dock Stowers, ordering these philanthropic emissaries off his farm. He wasn't about to trust his Republican backside to the dubious care of a bunch of Democrats!

Captain of the Head

A few years later, on the island of Guam, doing fealty to my country in the Navy, I found my outhouse training gave me an advantage over the sophisticated city boys, for plumbing (along with Lucky Strike green) hadn't gone to war, and the same old tannery structure was used here.

That was for number two, of course. For number one there were projecting metal tubes here and there, and in our parlance were christened wee-wee pipes.

The Navy had a name for its shack out back: head. One platoon leader gladdened the heart of a green boot by making him "Captain of the Head."

Which brings me to one final word. Did you hear about the Navajo boy who, after going away to college, returned with his diploma and an electric razor for his dad, and suddenly remembered there was no electricity in the town? He installed a dynamo, and thus became the first Indian to wire a head for a reservation.

JIM COMSTOCK
August 27, 1987

Dedication of Roosevelt's Backhouse

(The following recollections are offered by a **West Virginia Hillbilly** *reader who wishes to remain anonymous—Lord knows why!)*

Jim mentioned the headline in the *Clarksburg Exponent* of 1940 concerning the dedication of the fifty-thousandth Roosevelt "bungalow." I remember reading that headline myself, and thinking, why don't we go to Uncle Boyd's and dedicate his Roosevelt backhouse! If the people in Clarksburg can have a banquet to do it, at least we can have a picnic in our town.

My suggestion snowballed, and soon the planning was complete. Thirty-eight of us got together at Uncle Boyd's, children, grandchildren and in-laws. There were ten of us first cousins, eleven of our children, and the rest were those who were brave enough to marry into the family. We came from Elkins, Pickens, Gassaway and Morgantown. Among the group were two professors and their families, one from Davis and Elkins College and one from West Virginia University.

One prudish cousin stayed at home and was shocked because her 'sainted mother' indulged in such a vulgar ceremony!

Uncle Boyd didn't know what to make of all the commotion over his taking advantage of the Rural Sanitation Program of the Franklin Delano Roosevelt years. He had

25

moved to a farm on top of the mountain when his wife left him, taking along their only child, a daughter whom he adored. He renounced women forever, but his relatives would not let him be a hermit. And here we were!

The Elkins cousins prepared the 'throne room' for the ceremonies. This was a two-holer. On one side hung a Sears and Roebuck Catalogue, and there was a spittoon. Also a verse about how one could chew and spit. On the other side there was a roll of toilet tissue, an ash tray (cigarettes were popular then) and the latest *Cosmopolitan* magazine.

The picnic was held beneath the grape arbor covering the path to the outhouse. The posts of the arbor were decorated with alternating streamers of toilet tissue and newspapers. We were called to dinner when one of the little boys pounded an upside-down wash tub with a large stick, and after a delicious picnic the ceremony began. One cousin was designated to christen the building. The cousin who was master of ceremonies presented her with a corsage of cabbage and grape leaves, with dangling corncobs. A bottle of beer hung from the roof. She tried in vain to break the bottle, but her husband came to the rescue. He pulled a bottle opener from his pocket and opened the bottle and drank the beer.

One Morgantown cousin was the chief speaker. He spent half the night before typing his speech on a roll of toilet paper. I cannot remember much of it, but it began, "We cannot dedicate, we cannot consecrate any more than those who have gone before us have so dedicated and so consecrated." Sound familiar?

I read an original poem which, thank heavens, I've lost. Another cousin recited James Whitcomb Riley's "The Passing of the Backhouse" to close the program. This was, I believe, the last time all the brothers and sisters were togeth-

er. Since this was 47 years ago, I will forever cherish the pictures we took that day. But there were no pictures of Roosevelt's bungalow.

It Wasn't the Coat, But What Was in It

Bob Stewart, as a little boy, was waiting for the workman to come out of the outhouse behind his home in Highcoal, West Virginia, so he could use it himself. But the man stayed and stayed. Finally the door opened, and the man motioned to him.

"Son," he said, "do you have a fishing pole I could borrow?"

Bob ran behind the house and came back with his cane pole, then watched as the man dropped the hook and line down the hole in the outhouse. After a few minutes the man snagged something and pulled it up through the hole, and Bob was surprised to see that it was the man's coat which had somehow fallen in. It was a mess. The man held it up gingerly, his face expressing consternation and determination at the same time.

The boy wanted to ask the man why he didn't just drop the smelly coat back into the hole and be done with it, but he didn't have to. The workman read his mind and explained. "It ain't the coat, son. I'd be happy to part with it. But there's a ham sandwich and a boiled egg in the pocket, and I'm starved to death!"

JOHN WARTLUF

Throwing Big Money After Little

Two men were using a two-holer at the same time. As one finished his visit and pulled up his trousers, a quarter fell from his pocket down the hole.

The man sitting watched in amazement as the other man

angrily tossed a twenty-dollar bill down the hole.

"What on earth did you do that for?" he asked.

"Hell," the man replied with disgust, "you don't want people to think you'd go down there for a lousy quarter, do you?"

JOHN WARTLUF

3

The Muses Visit the Outhouse

The Passing of the Backhouse
JAMES WHITCOMB RILEY

When memory keeps me company
And moves to smiles or tears
A weather-beaten object
Looms through the mist of years.

Behind the house and barn it stood,
A half-mile or more,
And hurrying feet a path had made
Straight to its swinging door.

Its architecture was a type
Of simple classic art,
But in the tragedy of life
It played a leading part.

And oft the passing traveler
Drove slow, and heaved a sigh,
To see the modest hired girl
Slip out with glances shy.

We had our posy garden
That the women loved so well,
I loved it, too, but better still
I loved the stronger smell

That filled the evening breezes
So full of homely cheer,
And told the night-o'ertaken tramp
That human life was near.

On lazy August afternoons
It made a little bower,
Delightful, where my grandsire sat,
And whiled away an hour.

For there the summer morning
Its very cares entwined,
And berry bushes reddened
In the streaming soil behind.

All day fat spiders spun their webs
To catch the buzzing flies
That flitted to and from the house
Where Ma was baking pies.

And once a swarm of hornets bold
Had built a palace there,
And stung my unsuspecting Aunt—
I must not tell you where.

Then Father took a flaming pole,
That was a happy day—
He nearly burned the building up
But the hornets left to stay.

When summer bloom began to fade
And winter to carouse,
We banked the little building
With a heap of hemlock boughs.

But when the crust was on the snow
And sullen skies were gray,
In sooth the building was no place
Where one would wish to stay.

We did our duties promptly,
There, one purpose sway'd the mind,
We tarried not nor lingered long
On what we left behind.

The torture of that icy seat
Could make a Spartan sob,
For needs must scrape the goose flesh
With a lacerating cob

That from the frost-encrusted nail
Was suspended by a string—
My father was a frugal man
And wasted not a thing.

When Grandpa had to "go out back"
And make his morning call,
We'd bundle up the dear old man
With a muffler and a shawl.

I knew the hole on which he sat—
'Twas padded all around,
And once I dared to sit there—
'Twas all too wide I found.

My loins were all too little
And I jackknived there to stay;
They had to come and get me out,
Or I'd passed away.

Then Father said ambition
Was a thing that boys should shun,
And I must use the children's hole
'Til childhood days were done.

But I still marvel at the craft
That cut those holes so true,
The Baby hole, and the slender hole
That fitted sister Sue.

That dear old country landmark;
I tramped around a bit,
And in the lap of luxury
My lot has been to sit.

But ere I die, I'll eat the fruit
Of trees I robbed of yore,
Then seek the shanty where
My name is carved upon the door.

I ween the old familiar smell
Will soothe my faded soul,
I'm now a man, but nonetheless
I'll try the children's hole.

An English Jingle

In days of old
When knights were bold
And paper wasn't invented
They used blades of grass
To wipe their arse
And went away contented.

The Interstate Is Coming through My Outhouse
H.G. JOHE AND R.C. BLANKINSHIP, JR.

I'm proud to live in West Virginny
Them other places can't compare with us
But now I must relate what is happening in our state
By gosh, it's really causing quite a fuss

CHORUS: Oh the Interstate is coming through my outhouse
They tell me I'm on their right-of-way
I'll sell today and I'll get rich
But my path will end at the highway ditch
I'm making my last visit there today

Granny said to cancel Sears & Roebuck
Tell Uncle Sam to hurry up our dole
With all this progress comin' we'll change to inside plumbin'
And shorten up our early morning stroll

Old Uncle Ben has got a case of miseries
A-hikin' to that outhouse makes him tired
But he'll be getting better, he'll be an inside setter
When they install that cesspool in our yard

CHORUS

Them engineers made forty-seven surveys
They said to put it there and that was that
They'll bring a big steamroller and flatten my two-holer
But I'll keep right on voting Democrat!

Some day...when I grow old...and kinda feeble
Some moonlit night I'll wake up feeling strange
I'll finish up my bath and stroll down my old path
And wake up in a great big interchange!

(End with CHORUS plus the tag: "'Cause I figure Ronald Reagan's here to stay!" Or substitute Reagan's name with any well-known figure of the day.)

The Call at Dusk

BOYD CARR

i remember the call at dusk   the run back
Blue Ridge Industrial School   & after dark
be 4 the pail went up stairs & the light on
never minded the duty down the fire escape
in the morning even with frost
the take out & the top on
flash light was little help when the wind blew
shadows were hard to control
this little boy sought relief in cracks

but
things out in the day time
smells   retribution   seduction   injustice collection
for 40 years
wrote it down in a long poem   showed it around
shelved it
the mountains were bigger then

i still listen 4 the rumble

New Privy with "Interior Decoration"

(The following letter was written in verse form by a miner of the Valley some time after the WPA had built a new privy for his family, and is taken from The Typhoid Exterminator, circa 1936.—B.E.W.)

Mr. Kresworth, I got complaint
'Bout one danged can of ten-cent paint
My wife she's bought it at your store
And now by gosh I'm plenty sore.

You see, last week the spring she come
And everything she's on the hum.
Do walls, do floors, do windows too,
She clean like mad, I tell you.

My wife she's awful clean and neat
So she buy paint for privy seat.
For one whole week we watch with eye
But goshdarned paint she no get dry!

My wife she's short and kinda fat,
And you can see just where she sat.
She got big ring—goes round complete
Where she sat down on privy seat.

I say to her, "It serves you right,
You try to be so doggone tight.
That ten-cent paint she no darn good,
She won't get dry on privy wood."

My daughter, too, get ring around
When on the seat she did sit down.
For one whole week, by gosh we wait,
And now we all got constipate.

My wife she got a sis, Marie,
She live with daughter, wife and me.
Last night I look where she sit down,
By gosh, she too got ring around.

I try to clean with turpentine,
She howl like wolf, she lose her mind.
I'm scared like hell most all the day,
The skin come off, but paint she stay.

Now, look, we don't know what to do,
You got to eat and some come through.
My wife she sit and cry and cry
Because that paint she won't get dry.

Now, Mr. Kresworth, I ask you
What the heck we going to do?
The privy seat he no get dry,
If we don't move we going to die.

Now don't you think we got complaint
For buying can of that danged paint?
I live long time but never see
A man what got so mad like me.

But when I think about that paint
By gosh, I'm hot—I almost faint,
For how can house be nice and neat
If paint won't dry on privy seat?

Lunar Mythology

*(Wayne V. Masterson, P.O. Box 193, Bull Shoals, AR 72619, has written
me to ask the origin of the crescent moon carved in outhouse doors. I
can't shed much light on this question, but here is a verse I copied from
an old book, which might offer part of an answer.—B.E.W.)*

Many and many a year ago, about 400 years B.C.
The Romans gazed at the moon above with a strange
 mythology.
They believed the moon was a goddess, a virgin maiden fair.
They named the goddess Diana and put a crescent moon in her
 hair.
The crescent became a symbol that stands for women kind
And so the symbol was handed down to the outhouse out
 behind.
The privy that has the quarter-moon carved in the door or side
Signifies that the fairer sex should only be inside.
It seems the men had a symbol, too, to keep on even par.
It represented Sol, the sun, with a circle or a star.
Throughout many years of use the sun symbol fell by the way
But the crescent moon still prevails to be used by all today.

The Sanctuary

ANONYMOUS

Beneath the spreading Doug-fir tree
The weathered outhouse stands,
A sanctuary where you're free
From labor's harsh demands.

Of all the city's luxuries,
Tile, porcelain and chrome,
None satisfies and gives relief
Like that fragrant shack back home.

ODE TO THE LITTLE BROWN SHACK
OUT BACK

Words and Music by
BILLY EDD WHEELER

Moderately bright

Verses:

C

1. They passed an or-d'ance in the town. They said we'd have to tear it
2. It was not so long a - go that I went trip - ping through the
3. I would hum a hap - py tune a - peep-in' through the quar - ter
4. It was not a cas - tle fair, but I could dream my fu - ture
5. It was-n't fan - cy built at all, we had news - pa-pers on the

G

down;   That lit - tle old shack out back so dear to me.
snow;   Out to that house be - hind my old hound dog.
moon;   As my dad - dy's kin had done be - fore.
there And build my cas - tles to the yel - low jack - et's drone.
wall.   It was air con - di - tioned in the win - ter time.

C   C7   F

Though the health de - part - ment said, Its day was o - ver and dead,
Where I'd sit me down to rest like a snow - bird on his
It was in that qui - et spot dai - ly cares could be for -
I could or - bit 'round the sun; Fight with Gen - 'ral Wash-ing -
It was just a hum - ble hut, But its door was nev - er

C   G   C

It will stand for - ev - er in my mem - o - ry.
nest And read the Sears and Roe - buck cat - a - logue.
got. It gave the same re - lief to rich and poor.
ton, Or be a king up - on a gold - 'en throne.
shut, And a man could get in - side with - out a dime.

Chorus:

C

Don't let 'em tear_____ that lit-tle brown build - ing down,__ Don't let 'em

G   C

tear_____ that pre - cious build - ing down,__ Don't let 'em tear____

that dear old build - ing down.____ For there's not an-oth - er

Am   F   G   1.2.3.4.   5.
                                  C   C

like it in the coun-try or the town.____ 2.   It   was   town.____
                                        3.   I   would
                                        4.   It   was
                                        5. It was - n't

ODE TO GRANNY
AND THE LITTLE BROWN SHACK
OUT BACK

Words and Music by
BILLY EDD WHEELER

Gran - ny, Gran - ny, God bless my Gran - ny.

Spoken: 1. When I got old enough to go out back, Like the
2. — I can see now it took somebody grand to
3. But that was Granny. She was never too old to

big folks to the little brown shack, Who was right there to
steady a boy by holding his hand and still let him feel like,
have some fun, or she could get you told. When God made her, I guess He

lead me back? Old Granny.
well, he was a man. 2. —
busted his mold on Granny. 3. But

Gran - ny, Gran - ny, God bless Gran - ny.

1. But let me get back to that little brown shed I was
2. I guess I was just about two and a half, And
3. You see, I had me a plan, My nerve was aroused As I
4. As I looked in, how my heart beat, gettin'
5. But to be more proper I'll call them chairs, And I

talkin' about, And you can strike me dead, if this ain't the truth. I was
wide awake as a big - eyed calf, So I got up and
slipped out just as quiet as a mouse And opened the door of that
ready to climb to the big folks' seat that seemed to tower a
got to the big one by climbing the stairs of piled up catalogs,

4

The Outhouse Is No Laughing Matter

Granddaddy Wheeler and the Importance of Being Regular

Old people talk a lot about their bowels.

That's natural, I guess, but I'd never thought about it until I went to West Virginia to bring my Granddaddy Wheeler back to North Carolina to spend Christmas with us. He was in his late eighties or early nineties.

I always thought of Granddad as an active man, a hearty eater, always cutting weeds, hoeing the garden, doing something, so I hardly noticed when he started slowing down. I guess when you slow down you don't eat as much and you don't go to the bathroom as much. That's why it surprised me when he went on and on about his bowels after spending the night with a friend in Beckley, West Virginia, where I'd stopped to visit with Ewel Cornett, one of my best buddies, who directed my outdoor drama *Hatfields and McCoys*.

"Had a bowel movement last night, Billy!" he exclaimed loudly, without any preamble or beating around the bush, as soon as we hit the turnpike heading south out of Beckley.

"That's good, Daddy," I said sluggishly, a little tired from staying up half the night talking with my buddy Ewel. To my surprise Granddad went on.

"I cain't remember when I had one last. I enjoyed it. I'd like to have more of 'em."

"That's good, Daddy," I said, amazed at how his eyes sparkled, how rested he looked, how bright and perky his whole bearing was compared to the listless, wore-out way I felt. He usually didn't get this excited over anything, unless it was religion. He did like to talk religion, especially the Bible and how it was interpreted by the likes of Oral Roberts, to whom he had sent twenty percent of his railroad retirement income monthly until he fell out with Oral over some theological point.

Being regular is as important as religion, I thought, considering the way Granddad looked this morning when he talked about it. But how much can you say about this particular subject without running out of things to say? Not much, right? Wrong.

"They just acted like they wanted to go," Granddad said, jarring me out of a daydream about Devil Anse Hatfield and his clan.

"Go where, Daddy? Who?"

"My bowels, Billy!"

"Oh, yeah. I forgot. You had a good 'un last night, huh?"

"I don't know what got into 'em," he said gleefully, "but they jist ra'red up and wanted to go. So I let 'em. I don't know why they done it, but, I declare, I liked it. I reckon it's all this stirrin' around." (He pronounced it "steerin'.")

His shock of white hair stood up like an old rooster's

comb on his high forehead. His collar was buttoned at the top and he wore his vest with the plaited dark-leather chain looped across it, attached to his railroad watch, the big white-faced Bulova snugged away in his vest pocket. I remembered that watch and that dark buttoned-up vest from long ago, when the vest would always be flecked with little brown dots of dried tobacco juice. He chewed Beech-nut forty or fifty years and couldn't quit until his second wife, Gussie, helped convert him. He could name the day "the Lord took the taste out of my mouth." Granddaddy Wheeler worked hard all his life and used to have to worry about feeding a big family and paying the bills. Now, with all his wives gone, and his housekeeper-companions, al-most all of his friends, and one of his children, his main worry was being regular.

When my father-in-law, Dr. Arthur Bannerman, came to visit us Christmas day he struck up a conversation with my granddad. "Did you enjoy your Christmas dinner, Mr. Wheeler?"

"I reckon. I ain't heared from it yet," he said dryly.

It was a fine Christmas, and the finest presents Granddad got were the joys of going to the bathroom on a renewed and more-or-less regular basis. He talked about it half the way back to West Virginia, as if it were a thing of wonder, not to be comprehended, only to be enjoyed.

Pat and Mike Ride a Bull Train

Pat and Mike hadn't been in this country too long before they started hearing about trains, so they decided they'd like to take a train ride.

But they'd never seen a train.

"They're great big mean-looking things," a mountaineer told them one day. "And you'll know it when you see one. They burn coal that heats the steam boilers that make 'em go, and they make a fearsome sound, hissin' and clickety-clackin'. Got a caboose at the tail-end. They's one due along pretty soon, so just jump on her and take a ride."

They waited on the tracks until this great big bull busted out of his pen and ended up running down the tracks, his eyes on fire, his big hoofs kicking up splinters when they hit the railroad ties, clickety-clacking. Pat and Mike got excited.

"Here she comes!" Mike said to Pat. "Right on time."

They jumped on that bull, Mike hanging on to the horns a-straddle of that big neck, Pat bouncing around on the rump he took for the caboose. It was a rough ride and pretty soon Pat got bumped off the rump, but managed to grab hold of the tail with his hands, his feet dragging over the ties and that bull's hind feet kicking him in the shins. He tried to pull back up, but just when his face got even with that bull's caboose-hole it winked at him and farted two or three times, singeing his eyebrows, and started squirting turds like steaming walnuts all over him. He didn't know if he liked this train-riding business one bit, especially the caboose section.

"Cut off the engine, Mike!" he yelled. "She's belching steam and blowing hot cinders in my eyes!"

Pat and Mike Ride a Real Train

Wasn't too long until Pat and Mike found out that riding real trains was a lot more comfortable than riding bulls.

On their first train ride they lived it up, spent a lot of money eating sauerkraut and weiners in the dining car, drinking lots of beer and smoking cigars. Pretty soon Pat needed to go to the bathroom. The conductor told him where it was, so he hurried back and stepped into the little room with its tiny metal sink and the lid down on the toilet. He figured it was a chair without a back where you sat to

look at yourself in the mirror. He couldn't decide where a man was supposed to go, but he knew he had to do something quick, for Mother Nature was calling him with a mighty urgent voice.

The window was open. "Ah," he said with satisfaction, "there it is, and it's air-conditioned!"

He dropped his pants and stuck his two half-moons out the window, and let her fly. Just then the train went through a tunnel, the walls of which were so close to the window it gave Pat's behind a good scraping.

When he joined Mike back in the passenger car Mike asked him how he liked it. "Oh, it was prime," he said. "First rate. They think of everything on these-here modern trains."

Mike noticed that he sat down kind of gingerly, though, and asked him about it.

"Oh, it's nothing," Pat said. "These trains have real nice bathrooms. But it's gonna take me a while to get used to them electric ass-wipers!"

Pat and Mike in the Hotel Room

After that abrasive train ride Pat needed some rest, so he and Mike decided to blow the rest of their money and rest up in a hotel.

It wasn't a fancy hotel. They didn't have bathrooms in the room, but there was one on each floor. That was okay, but sometimes you couldn't get into the bathroom when you needed to.

That night after eating beans and onions and German sausages and red cabbage, cornbread and buttermilk and peach cobbler, Mike had to go in the worst way. He ran down the hall, but the bathroom was occupied. He waited and waited, then went back to the room. "Pat," he said, "I've got to go! I can't wait no longer."

Pat was the resourceful one. An idea struck him. "Go in your sock. Then sling it out the window. Nobody'll know the difference."

Mike thought that was a wonderful notion. He took his big sock, filled it up, then slung it round and round, aiming to throw it out the window. But the sock had a hole in it. The payload ended up splattered around the walls and all that went out the window was an empty sock.

The next day the maid assigned to clean up their room looked at the walls in disgust. She called another maid into the room and said, "Just look at this mess! Have you ever seen anything like it? I'm a good mind to call the manager and report them two Irishmen."

Her friend was more philosophical. She looked at the walls in wonder, said, "Honey, I'd just like to know how a man can get his ass in a position to do something like that. I'd give a hundred dollars just to a-seen that!"

John Wayne Toilet Paper

This Indian came into the trading post one day and bought a lot of supplies. He was a penny-pincher, so he told the proprietor he wanted some toilet paper, asked what did he have.

"Well, I got some deluxe paper here, two-ply, white, extra soft, and it costs 99 cents a roll. It's called Soft as Clouds."

"Ugh," the Indian grunted, "too much. Want'um paper more cheap."

"Well," the storekeeper said, "here's a nice single-ply, yellow, medium grade. It's 64 cents a roll. They call this one Darling's Delight."

"Still too much," the tight Indian said. "Need'um better deal. What else you got'um?"

The trading post man said, "Well, I've got a special on

this week. I've got some paper at 37 cents a roll."

"Hmmm! Good. What you call'um this one?"

"It ain't got a name. It's just paper."

The Indian said, "Indian have name for everything. We name'um. You wait see." And he bought a good supply of the no-name paper. In a month or two he was back at the trading post to buy more supplies. "John Wayne toilet paper no good," he said right off. "No like'um, no buy."

The clerk asked him why he named it John Wayne toilet paper?

"Because," the Indian said gravely, "it's white, rough as cob, and it don't take no shit off the Indians!"

BETSY KAHL
Swannanoa, N.C.

One Pill Every Four Hours

This mountain man was so constipated he didn't know what to do.

He took prunes by the pound, Ex-Lax by the bar, and castor oil by the bottle, but nothing would loosen him up. He was driving everybody crazy with his sour disposition. His wife, tired of his pinched face and ill temper, finally made him go to the doctor in Asheville.

The doctor examined him and gave him a prescription guaranteed to create some action. After getting his bottle of pills from the druggist he was driving home and decided to stop and take some of his medicine, but he couldn't remember whether the man told him to take one pill every four hours or four pills every hour. He was bound to have relief, he wasn't taking any chances, so he took four pills every hour. Used up the whole bottle by bedtime.

The next morning his son came running up to the house, his face pale and full of foreboding, and yelled, "Ma! Ma, Daddy's sitting down there in the outhouse, and he looks like...Ma, he looks like he's dead!"

"He is dead, honey," she said. "We're gonna bury him soon as he quits shittin'."

A Few Quotes

A fart is the sharpest thing in the world. It can cut through your pants and not leave a mark.

I.P. SNOWFLAKE

I ate so many frog legs during the war, every time I'd take a shit it'd get up and hop away.

A CONFEDERATE
SOLDIER

Be careful of letting the cat pee on the cash register. It could run into money!

BRUD SHELTON
Hazard, Kentucky

I think I'll flush myself down the john and commit sewer-cide.

U.N. KERMODE

Hemorrhoids are like Yankees. You don't mind if they come down every now and then, and go back. But when they come down and hang around too long they can get to be a pain in the ass.

I.C. DOOALOT

A fartin' horse will never tire,
A fartin' man's the man to hire!

JERRY CHESNUT
Nashville, Tennessee

Pa Got Cold-Nosed and Sixteen Chickens Died

My fishing buddy, Charlie Stafford, hadn't been around for a while, so I asked him why.

"Been pluckin' chickens," he said in his best hillbilly twang. (Fact is, nobody talks hillbilly like Charlie. He sounds like Festus and Gomer and all the TV hillbillies rolled into one. But he's the real ar-tickle, as he would say it himself.)

"Pap killed a passel of chickens t'other nite. Never seed so many chicken feathers. I been eatin' fried chicken, baked chicken, chicken'n'dumplin's, chicken in them-ere castor-rolls, chicken ever-which-a-way."

I asked him why they killed so many chickens all at once.

"You know how a dog's nose is allus cold?" he said, sneaking up on the story, which is the way Charlie always tells a story, never just in a straight line. "Well, our dog Blue is the worst-un fer it ever was. We'd been losin' a few chickens at night, and Pap figured the job fer a weasel. But them weasels is slick. They git in and git out.

"Pap set a lantern in a corner of the chicken house and took to totin' his shotgun to the outhouse wif him of a nite, jist to have it handy, don't ye know. Pap's a good hand fer goin' to the privy at nite, 'specially at apple time like it is now.

"Well, t'other nite he ambled out to the outhouse to set and take him a good rest, when he heared a commotion in the chicken house. He grabbed up his shotgun, didn't take time to button up the back flap to his long-handles, went sneakin' up, opened that leetle side door and stuck in the gun. You know it's got a hair trigger. Jist when he leaned over to have a look, Blue come up behind him in the dark and cold-nosed him!"

Hershey Kisses on the Privy Seat

Charlie lives out here at Black Mountain, North Carolina, and when he ain't plucking chickens, why, he's a fix-it man of the highest order. If it hums, purrs, rotates, rolls, gurgles, chugs, heats or cools he can fix it...anything from a bulldozer to a cigarette lighter. I never dreamed he knew anything about outhouses, though.

Once he even rewired my recording studio, took out a module of the mixing board and rebuilt it, replacing condensers, circuitry, faders and equalizers and tracked down several static crackles in the lines between the board and the speakers. I asked him how he did it, being a fix-it man and plumber?

"'Lectricity is jist like water," says he, "it comes in hyar and goes out thar. You jist figure out where she's a-leakin' and stop her up."

"Where do you reckon you get this gift from?" I asked.

"From my Pap," he said. "He used to be the best outhouse builder in Buncombe County, a-fore he took in to mechanickin'."

When I told Charlie I was writing a book about outhouses, his eyes lit up and he chuckled, making his big belly shake. "Shucks, Pap built the purtiest privies you ever laid a eyeball on. And he didn't jist build 'em, he garn-teed 'em. When I'as jist a tow-headed whippersnapper he took me on a complaint job. Now, Pap didn't get many complaints, and in this par-tiklar case he had to step easy, 'cause it was old Miss Gilmartin, the schoolteacher.

"See, she wouldn't come right out and say what the trouble was. Pap sorter had to go at her delicate-like...you know, read 'tween the lines. All she'd tell him was, it was *irritatin'*. Or she'd say it *surprised* her at times. When he pumped her fer details she jist blushed and walked away, sayin', 'You inspect it carefully . . . uh, very closely and you'll see.'

"That didn't give him much to go on, but he figured if the roof was leakin' she'd say so. If the door latch was sprung or the door wasn't swingin' right, she'd tell him that, too. So he narr'ed it down. It had to be the seat. Pap run his fingers round and round. It was smooth as a rat runnin' through cotton. Or it seemed to be, to the touch. He stuck his bearded face down close to the front edge of that-t'ere seat and when he raised up he said *ouch!*

"He smiled right big. One of his chin whiskers'd caught in a teeny crack. 'Thar's the trouble!' he said. 'Reckon that would surprise a lady ever' now and agin. Smarts, too.' He got out his sandpaper and had that seat fixed in a jiffy."

The Ultimate Outhouse

Like the man said one time, you can search the world over looking for diamonds, then come back home and find them in your own back yard. I'd been writing people all over the country for outhouse stories, and here was a mother lode, stored up in the memory of my best fishing buddy, Charlie.

All I had to do was ask. And Charlie went on:

"Pap could a-been content buildin' outhouses, 'cause he was partial to 'em, but he had to carpenter on school-houses, churches, cabins, reg'lar houses to, you know, make a livin'. Then in the late thirties an' early forties outhouses commenced losin' out to indoor johns. People used privies fer storage shacks, let 'em grow up in weeds. Made Pap sad to see it.

"Lordy, he took pride in his work. He could build ye a caddy-lac of a privy, or a Ford Pinto. And he knowed when to go fer comfort or when to aim fer practical-ness. Fer in-stance, if a body liked to linger and read the paper, Pap built 'em fer easy settin'. Iffen they'as built fer a sawmill where the boss didn't want his hands loafin' in there too

long, why, he left the seats ruff-cut...jist sawed out the holes, hit 'em a lick or two with a rasp.

"He knowed where to place 'em to catch the best light, and still be private, and how high to make the seats, which kind of roofs worked best, and all that stuff. Pap was a master of his trade. He studied it all out, ye see."

I asked Charlie what kind of outhouse his father favored for his own use.

"We had a one-holer with a half-moon ventilator, a door that swung in so's to keep somebody from catchin' ye at yer biz-ness. And Pap loved a tin roof. You can see up through the leetle nail holes, but it's funny, the rain don't never leak down through them holes. He never used knotty boards, 'cause he said knotholes'd either fall out on ye or somebody'd poke 'em out, and there ye'd be, never knowin' if ye'as bein' spied on. Man cain't go proper if he's got a notion somebody's a-watchin'. He had a place fer stackin' Sears & Roebuck catalogues and a box fer corn cobs. And he had a ten-pound lard bucket full of lime, fer sprinklin', ye know.

"Pap favored the settin' sun over sunrises, so our outhouse faced west. Nothin' pleasured him more than to take the *Asheville Citizen-Times* and sit there a-readin' and watchin' that ole sunball sinkin' slowly behind Mount Pisgah and the Rat, with bees a-buzzin' in the sourwoods and the peepers peepin' down on Lake Tomahawk, callin' fer rain. Peaceful, it was. That was livin'. You cain't do that

with indoor plumbin'. Fer a long time, before I could read, I thought newspapers was a laxative, 'cause Pap'd never go to the outhouse 'thout takin' along his paper. And, of course, iffen he read somethin' he didn't like or didn't agree with, he knowed what to do with it. He tore it out, rubbed it 'tween his hands to soften it up, then put it behind him...outta sight and outta mind."

Charlie told me lots of outhouse stories. But the one I liked best was the one he told on himself.

"Pap was really par-tiklar 'bout keepin' his privy clean. When I was knee-high to a grasshopper sometimes he'd get after me when I scooted down offen his seat, an' he'd say, 'You ain't been leavin' them little doots on the edge of my seat, have ye?'"

I'd never heard that word before, so I asked Charlie, "What in the world is a doot?"

He laughed that loud belly-shaking laugh and smiled mischievously at me. "Ah," he said, "it's jist a leetle ole brown thing that swirls out to a sharp point. Looks like one of them Hershey kisses."

An Odd-Tasting Apple Butter

One time this traveling salesman was having a good run and found himself way out in the country at dark, too tired to drive back to town. So he found a friendly farmhouse where they put him up for the night.

It was cold that January night. The notion came over him

to go to the outhouse, but when he opened the back door and looked out at the path that led to the outhouse, icy wind and rain made him step back inside with a shiver.

The hallway that led to the back door had shelves on each side, stacked high with canned goods. He looked at those jars. He looked outside. And once again necessity was the mother of invention. He found an empty quart jar, went in it, screwed the lid back on tight and set it high on the shelf where he didn't think it would be noticed. Next morning, he thought, he would take that jar to the outhouse and empty it and nobody would be the wiser.

But he forgot. He was clean back to town before he remembered, thirty miles away, and the roads were freezing slick. So he decided to wait and take care of the matter the next time he was out that way.

About a month later the farmer's daughter walked into the kitchen licking her finger and holding that quart jar at arm's length.

"Hey, Maw," she said, with her eyebrows squinched down to the bridge of her wrinkled nose, "you know that apple butter you said tasted like shit? Well...hit-twere!"

Hemorrhoids and the Glass Eye

This man had such a bad case of hemorrhoids the doctor set a date for him to have surgery.

It worried him to death. By the time the day before the surgery rolled around, he was a basket case. He thought

he'd call the doctor and make an excuse not to have it done. But his wife talked him out of it, said he had to face the music some day, so he might as well get it over with.

He agreed, but it worried him so much he decided to go get drunk, so that evening he went down to his favorite local bar. It was a real smoky place and he got to rubbing his eyes, one of which was a glass eye, but he rubbed them both to keep people from thinking he only had one eye. As he rubbed his eyes one time, he leaned forward to pick up his drink, and that glass eye fell into his drink. He didn't realize he'd lost it for a minute, and by that time he'd chug-a-lugged his drink and ordered another.

He'd swallowed his glass eye! Now he was in a quandary. But after a few more drinks he settled down and reasoned that since he was already going to the doctor tomorrow, he'd see about it then.

The next day the doctor bent him over and spread his cheeks to have a look, saw that eye looking back at him, raised up in a huff, said, "Now, looky here, if you don't trust me, just go find yourself another doctor!"

The Strange New Water Closet

Right after the turn of the century a man was heard speaking down at the local barber shop in Kansas City. He was normally a reserved man, yielding the floor to the more aggressive and loud yarn-spinners, but today he was wound up. He was excited. And his audience was all ears listening to him tell his story:

"My wife sent off to Monkey Wards for one of them new-fangled things called a water closet. Or was it Sears and R'ar Back? Anyhow, the whole kit-and-kabootle is called a bathroom, and let me tell you boys, is it ever fancy!

"Now, it has to be in-stalled by a man called a plummer. On one side of the room is a big long thing that looks like a hog-trough, except it's smooth, and that's where you get in and waller around and wash yourself all over. On the other side of the room is a little white thing called a sink, with a stopper in the bottom. This is where you take your 'possible baths.' You know, you wash up as far as possible, or you wash down as far as possible, and if nobody's looking, why, you hit ole possible a lick or two.

"But, now, I'll tell you what takes the cake. The foot-washer! Fellers, it sits over in the corner and you ain't never seen a contraption like it. Why, you put in one foot and wash it, then pull this chain, and, swoosh! you've got clean water for the other foot.

"Two lids came with that foot-washer, and I'm danged if we can figure out what they're for. So we're using one for a bread board, and the other one, the one that had a big hole in it, we used that one to frame Grandpa's picture with. And I'll tell you something, now, that company is on the ball. They're fine folks to do business with. They sent us a whole roll of writing paper with it, free of charge!"

A Mighty Fine Cream Cheese

This fellow dropped in on his buddy one evening to have a beer, and he was asked if he would like to have some cheese and crackers. After sampling the cheese, then eating it all, he said, "By golly, that sure was good cheese. Where did you buy it?"

His buddy said, "I didn't buy it, I made it." When asked how he did it, he said, "Simple. I took an old sock, filled it with thick cream, and hung it out in the shithouse for a month or two to season."

A few months later the visit was reversed. The buddy was asked if he would like a beer with some cheese and crackers. After drinking a few beers and eating all the cheese, he asked the friend where he bought that excel-

lent cheese? "I didn't buy it," he said. "I made it just like you did. I took an old sock, filled it with shit and hung it in the cream house for a month or two to season."

EDW. LOWE, inventor
of Kitty Litter®
Cassopolis, Mich.

The Storm

A young fellow was courting the daughter of a very prominent family. They were being served tea and biscuits in the parlor by the butler. A small poodle lay at the young lady's dainty feet, sleeping.

Unfortunately the young man had to break wind. So he asked the girl if she would like to hear his new piano composition, called "The Storm."

She nodded, so he went quickly to the baby grand piano and played very well. Each time he had to fart he would hammer loudly on the bass keys, imitating thunder. He did this about four times.

A little later he asked her if she would like to hear "The Storm" again?

"Yes," she replied sweetly, picking up the poodle who was sniffing the air, and stroking his fur, "but this time, if you please, leave out the part where the lightning strikes the shithouse!"

EDW. LOWE

A Biased Opinion

Two men stood at the urinal side by side in the airport men's room in Lexington, Kentucky.

One man looked sideways at the other, said, "I'll bet you're from Cincinnati."

The other man was quite surprised, said, "Why, yes, as a matter of fact I am. How in the world did you know?"

"There's a rabbi there who cuts on the bias," the man said, "and you're pissing in my shoe."

Wish I'd Said That (But Mickey Mantle Beat Me to It)

Several years ago I was playing golf in Red Steagal's Celebrity golf tournament at a Byron Nelson course in the rolling hill country of Texas. As usual, there was a "guitar pullin'" after the practice round the first day.

Alex Harvey was there, with his buddy, Coach Darrell Royal, and Charley Pride, Willie Nelson, several Nashville songwriters and their buddies. We passed the guitar around until the wee hours of the night, telling jokes between songs. Sitting quietly in the corner until the last song was sung and the last joke told was one of my heroes, Mickey Mantle.

As we left the smoky room Mickey, an unassuming, almost shy man, shook my hand and told me he enjoyed my songs. When he was out of earshot somebody told me that Mickey was a really fine golfer and a hard-core country music fan.

He said Mickey was always a gentleman. Said, "Once he was using the john in a crowded men's room, sitting in a stall next to a man who was really stinking up the place. It was almost unbearable. (I'd been in that situation before, but never knew what to say or had the guts to say it. But Mickey did.) Mickey addressed the man's visible feet, said gently, 'Hey, buddy, how about a courtesy flush!'"

Spring Water on the Train

A West Virginia mountaineer was taking his first train ride to Charleston, and he was powerful thirsty. He'd no sooner sat down when he asked his wife to go get him a drink. She hurried off and came back with a paper cup full of water, which he drank, but it was a small cone-shaped cup and the man said, "Get me another, please."

This time she came back empty-handed, said to her husband, "Sorry, you'll have to wait a minute—there's a man sitting on the spring."

The Pipe Smoker

Outhouses have for a long time provided not only a place of respite and meditation, but also a place to sneak a smoke. Normally this was not a dangerous thing to do, but there are a few stories of outhouses catching on fire, singeing bottoms and causing general embarrassment, and in a few cases even exploding.

These mishaps have been near-fatal.

Like the cautious North Carolina housewife who once bought a gallon of naphtha to use in her spring cleaning. After finishing her work, she found that she had about a half gallon of the naphtha left over. Afraid to leave the volatile stuff in the house and risk a fire or explosion, she took it out back and poured it down a hole in the privy.

Her old man had occasion to go to the outhouse a few minutes later. He settled down, filled his pipe, lit it and prepared to enjoy a private smoke.

He raised up and dropped the match down the hole under him. Instantly there was a great explosion, blowing out the sides of the johnny-house, lifting the roof into orbit over the large oak tree, and bodily throwing the old man into a manure pile fifty feet away. The housewife screamed and neighbors came running. They dug the man out, examined him for broken bones and other injuries.

Except for being stunned, and dazed, the old man seemed to be all right. Someone asked him how it happened.

"I dunno," said the old man, "it must a-been somethin' I et."

A "Definite" Surprise

In a country schoolroom somewhere in Appalachia the teacher asked her class to make up a sentence using the word "definitely."

Immediately a little girl's hand went up. "Teacher, teacher," she said with enthusiasm, "the sky is definitely blue."

"Not necessarily," the teacher corrected her. "Sometimes the sky is red, or pink, or even green or brown."

Another girl's hand shot up. "Teacher, teacher!...The grass is definitely green." Again the teacher replied patiently. "No, dear, sometimes the grass is yellow, parched by drought and sun, and sometimes it is brown. In Kentucky in some places it even looks blue. Anybody else?"

There was a long silence, the kids afraid to jump in and give hasty examples, having seen two good sentences shot down. Finally a little boy rose with a cautious, quizzical look on his face. "Teacher," he began shyly, but bravely, "when ye fart is they supposed to be a lump in it?"

The teacher blushed, a little angry at the boy's question, but put off by his sincere demeanor, decided to ignore his crudity. "Well, no, I suppose not."

The boy said, "Well, then...I have *definitely* shit!"

STEVE CLARK
Big Hill, Ky.

Some Initial Confusion

A newly married couple rented a house out in the country, and after moving in, the young wife noticed that the bathroom did not have a commode. She decided to write the landlord about it. Being extremely modest, however, she could not bring herself to write the words bathroom commode, so she used the initials B.C., feeling sure the landlord would know what she meant.

When the landlord got the letter he was puzzled, but felt that surely the young lady meant Baptist Church, so he wrote her as follows:

Dear Madam:

In reply to your letter, there is a nice little B.C. about four and a half miles down the road toward town that will seat 250 people. That might seem pretty far, if you are in the habit of going regularly, but you will no doubt be glad to know that many people take their lunch and make a day of it. They usually arrive early and stay late. The last time my wife and I went, last year, we were a little late, so we had to stand up. This did not bother me as I am in the habit of standing a lot, but the ladies don't seem to like it. It was particularly uncomfortable for my wife as she has arthritis in both knees.

It may interest you to know that a box supper is planned

in the near future to raise funds to buy new, plusher seats. A very friendly usher always greets you on arrival at the B.C. and takes you to your seat. Years ago men and women did not sit together there, but in these modern times they sit and meditate together.

Many people do not go except on Thanksgiving, Christmas, and Mother's Day. It is sad that folks don't go more often, and don't do much when they do go. It pains me very much that I don't go more often, myself, but it is certainly not a lack of desire on my part. As I grow older it is more of an effort, especially in cold weather. In closing, let me say that I hope to see you there soon. In fact, I could come and go with you the first time you go, and introduce you to the others there, if you'd like.

Sincerely,
Your Landlord

OPIE C. COBB,
Middleport, Oh.;
C.C. ALBAUGH,
Buckhannon, W. Va.;
ROSE MICHEL,
Wheeling, W. Va.

His First Visit to an Outhouse

The following is a true story:

In the early '70s my daughter and grandson and I were coming from Washington, D.C. to Charleston, West Virginia. It was on a Sunday and I was about to run out of gas. I stopped at a little country service station, and my grandson, about four years old, wanted to use the bathroom. The people said all they had was an outhouse. My daughter (Veneta) and my grandson (Jay) went and used it.

When they returned Veneta was laughing. I asked her what she was laughing about? She said, "Jay wanted to know how you flush that thing!"

OPIE C. COBB

Even a Blind Man Could Find It

For many years there was an old wooden "crapper" out in the field on the late Evan Jones's Ranch, twelve miles northwest of Riverside, Washington. It used to get quite "ripe," and when the wind was blowing in the right direction, even a blind man could find it. The odor would keep a skunk or a mad hornet at bay!

WALT THAYER
Wenatchee, Wash.

"Going to See Aunt Maggie"

A young lady in the Wenatchee area operated a million-dollar piece of construction equipment. The company was very cost-efficiency-minded, so they installed a portable toilet right on the machine, so she wouldn't have to shut down the big machine while she "went to see Aunt Maggie."

WALT THAYER

Rattlesnakes and Snowballs

I recall a railroad foreman who went out in the sagebrush to "set out a bad order" (that's R.R. slang), but soon came hurrying back with his overalls at half-mast and said, "Just as I got squatted down I discovered a rattlesnake, right under my fanny!"

When he went later to make his deposit, he made sure

the area was clear of rattlers.

Now, if you want to give your fanny the ultimate in abuse, just use a snowball to wipe with, or a pine cone, or accidentally use some burning nettles or poison oak. The latter is worst of all, and you'll have a genuine "sore keister."

Well, as the old sailor would say, "'Blow all hands aft.'"

WALT THAYER

A "Dirty Trick" on Halloween

One bad trick some fellows used to play on Halloween night was moving the outhouse backward about three feet, then covering the hole with a sheet of tin, which was covered with dirt. In the dark you couldn't see the trap, and when you went in feet-first you not only got the s—t scared out of you, you got a lot of it on you. That's what I call a dirty, stinking trick.

WALT THAYER

Tipping Over Toilets Was "Big Business"

For several years somebody always tipped over the toilets at the country school on Halloween night. Nobody knew who did it, but they noticed that every time it happened a nearby farmer always had a team of horses handy to come and tip them up again. Those three-holers were heavy.

Eventually they discovered that it was the farmer himself who tipped them over, because he was paid five dollars to set them up again, and he was enjoying a pretty good business. After he was found out, the toilets were never bothered again on Halloween night.

WALT THAYER

Mama Was Blue in the Face

A geologist came to visit this poor Texas dirt farmer, told him he thought there was reason to believe there might be oil or gas on his land and, if he didn't mind, they would drill a hole to find out. He said, "If there's as much oil down there as we think, you'll be a rich man. A very rich man." Of course the farmer told them to go ahead.

They drilled and drilled, going down through dirt and sand, shamrock and shale, limestone...down, down, down for a thousand feet. But they never did strike oil or gas. So the geologist said to the farmer, "I guess we struck out. I'm sorry. We'll just put a cap over that deep hole and move on."

The farmer looked over at his outhouse and got a sudden inspiration. "Hey, wait a minute!" he said. "See that outhouse yonder? I've moved that thing several times...it's hard work. Why don't you take that big crane of yours, lift that outhouse up, and set it down over that thousand-foot hole? Why, I'd never have to move that thing again!"

The geologist had his men set the outhouse over the hole, and they left. Next morning the farmer's son came running to the house, very excited, said, "Pap! I'm afraid Mama's dead or something. She's sitting down there in the outhouse with this strange look. Her face has turned blue, her eyes are bugged out, and the veins of her neck are standing out like banjer strings. You better come quick!"

The farmer chuckled, said, "Don't worry, son, your mama's okay. She just likes to hold her breath 'til she hears it hit bottom."

JIMMY DEAN,
country singer and
sausage entrepreneur
Ft. Lauderdale, Fl.

Of Outhouses and Cherry Trees

One time at Halloween Jack Barlow and some of his buddies had run out of ideas for making mischief, they'd pulled tricks on people all night, so they were just about to quit and go to bed when they decided that one more rusty wouldn't hurt. So they pushed over the two-holer behind Jack's house. It was a cold, crisp night and the frost was on the pumpkin. That outhouse made one heck of a splash when it rolled off the bank into the Big Coal River. Jack figured that by morning it would be floating down the Kanawha, heading for the Ohio and eventually the mighty Mississippi itself. They slapped each other on the back, thinking that was a nice piece of work!

Next morning Jack's daddy snatched him out of bed by his ear. He looked awful cross, like he'd tangled with a chain saw and lost. He said, "Now, Jack, I'm gonna ask you a question and, by grabs, I want the truth. Was you with them boys that pushed over our outhouse last night...into that cold, cold river? I thought I recognized your laugh." Jack knew he was in bad trouble, but he remembered his history and decided to make a brave show of it.

"Well, Daddy," he said, "just like George Washington...I can't tell a lie. Yes, sir, I was with 'em." With that Mr. Barlow took off his belt and commenced to blister Jack's sitting-down place pretty good with it. Jack protested: "When George Washington cut down the cherry tree and told the truth about it, his daddy didn't whip him. He let him go!"

"Yeah," Mr. Barlow said, "and I don't reckon George's daddy was *in* that cherry tree when he chopped it down, neither!"

The Little Boy Who Swallowed a Bullet

This woman that lived up on Cooger's Branch came tearing out of the holler one day with her little boy, drove to the doctor's office, rushed into the room, and declared, "Doctor, Doctor, my boy Elmer, here, has swallered a .22 shell! What are we gonna do?"

The doctor calmed her down, assured her Elmer would be all right, told her, "Just take him back home and feed him a bottle of castor oil, and...don't aim him at nobody!"

The Dog Got the Blame

This country boy was sitting in the swing with his girl-friend, hugging and kissing up a storm, when he had a sudden attack of gas. He fought to hold it in, not wanting to embarrass himself *or* to break the spell of the good sugar he was enjoying.

Just then the girl's dog walked up on the porch and laid down right under the swing where they sat. That dog gave the boy an idea. He raised up on one cheek and snuck out a long, satisfying fart, then looked down at the dog and said, "Rover! Shame on you. Now, you quit that."

The boy went on a-courting hot and heavy, but before long he had another gas attack, so he slipped another one out and said, harshly but good-naturedly too, "Now Rover, dang you, you cut that out!" It made him smile inside, he was so proud of himself for thinking up such a good idea. After he'd repeated his trick several more times he was surprised when his girl pulled back during a long, juicy kiss and said, "Honey, the dog left a long time ago, and I'm afraid if you ain't careful you're a-gonna shit your britches!"

It's a Little Cloudy, Ain't It?

A man was in the hospital following an operation.

One day the nurse came by and left a specimen bottle, told the man, "We need to do a urinalysis on you. Go some for me in that bottle and I'll be back later to pick it up."

He decided to have some fun, so he filled the up with some leftover tea he'd had for lunch. When the nurse came back she picked up the bottle, held it up to the light, said, "It's a little cloudy, ain't it?"

"I don't know," the man said seriously, "let me see it."

He drank it all down and the nurse fainted!

One Hell of an Earache

A friend of mine, Jerry Brackett, had a mild case of hemorrhoids and he made it worse "clipping off the cling-ons from the planet Uranus," as he called it in his colorful way of speaking. He thought doctors were overpaid and prided himself on taking care of things himself, like putting spells on warts or tying threads around them until they dropped off.

But he got a bad earache, and nothing he could do would make it go away, so he broke down and went to see the old country doctor. The doctor examined him. Then told him to go home and bring him back a urine specimen.

"That old quack," he muttered on the way home. "What's a urine specimen got to do with an earache?"

So he thought he'd just *show* that doctor.

He found a small coffee can and let his wife pee in it, then his grandmother...even got his dog to add a few squirts to it, and then he topped it off himself. Took it back, thinking, "Now, let's see what he can make out of that!"

The doctor took Jerry's coffee can back to his lab and analyzed its contents. Pretty soon he came back out. "Your dog's got a bad case of the mange," he said, with a sly but matter-of-fact air. "Your wife's got sugar in the blood, your granny's slightly anemic, and if you don't quit taking your nail clippers to your hemorrhoids you're gonna end up with one hell of an earache!"

Granddad Yelled "Fire"

One evening this farmer moved his outhouse to a new location, a good ways out the path from the house, and since it was so late he figured he could wait until morning to cover the old hole.

But that night Granddad felt the urge, walked out the path in the dark, and fell in...up to his chin. "Fire! Fire!" he yelled at the top of his lungs. Here came his son, the farmer, just a-running, with his wife and their two children. They pulled Granddad out of his predicament and were hosing him down good, relieved that there was no fire.

"We're sure glad you're okay, Granddaddy," the farmer said, "but tell me something. Why on earth did you holler *'fire'?*"

The old man said, "I needed help in a hurry. And I wasn't sure you'd come a-runnin' quite as fast if I hollered *'shit'!*"

JIMMY DEAN

The Boy Who Liked Cokes

This one little boy liked fountain cokes so much that every afternoon he'd come to the drugstore, hop up on a stool, and say, "Gimme a coke-coke-e-doke!"

It was cute for a while, but the waitress got tired of it day after day, so one afternoon she saw him coming and decided she'd cure him of his little ritual. She poured a glass half full of castor oil and filled it on up with coke. When he hopped up on the stool and said, "Gimme a coke-coke-e-doke!" she served him that slick special. He drank it down and went on home.

She didn't see the boy for several days. But it wasn't long until here he came, cheerful as ever, and hopped up on the stool. "Gimme a coke-coke-e-doke," he said, "uh...without the poop-poop-e-doop!"

LARRY SMITH
Swannanoa, N.C.

Out of Corn Cobs

A man wrote to Sears & Roebuck: "Dear Sirs, would you please send me two large sacks of corn cobs. My money order is enclosed."

Sears wrote the man back: "Dear Sir, if you will look on page 44 of our new catalogue, you will see that we no longer stock this item."

The man wrote back: "Dear Mr. Sears & Roebuck...shucks, if I had your catalogue, I wouldn't need the corn cobs. But thanks, anyway."

*In the Middle of Shakespeare's **Hamlet***

During World War II these two mountain boys were stationed in England, and one evening they decided to go see Shakespeare's *Hamlet* at the Royal Academy, or some such fancy place.

They'd drunk a lot of beer at the NCO club just before going to the theater, so during the play one said to the other, "Where do you reckon their outhouse is? I gotta go."

"Sshhh," his buddy whispered. "Wait 'til this act is over."

"I cain't! I'm about to bust. I gotta go *now.*"

"Now, look," the buddy told him, "these English folks take their Shakespeare serious, and we're just gettin' to that famous 'to be or not to be' speech. You better not get up now and make a ruckus."

But to-go-or-not-to-go, that was the question in that mountain soldier boy's mind, and to-go was ahead by three or four beers. He was desperate. "Okay," his buddy told him, "but, I swear, I don't think you better get up. You'll get us both killed. Look, we're on the front row of the balcony. Just dangle your hose over the edge and go. Nobody'll even notice, they're so wrapped up in this play."

So he did. He unzipped old Buford and let him go over the balcony, sighing with relief. Presently an old English gent in the audience below stood up and, wiping his brow with his handkerchief, addressed the soldier above him.

"I say, old fellow," he said, in a voice full of dignity and forbearance, "would you mind waving it about a bit? I seem to be getting the bulk of it!"

The Drunk Who Missed His Shorts

A traveling salesman asked for a room in a rural hotel and was told that they were full up. It was late and the poor man was weary. "Are you sure you haven't got a room...*anything?*"

The hotel clerk shook his head, but the salesman looked so forlorn, he thought a minute and said, "We've got this drunk, a regular customer, who wouldn't mind if you shared his room, I'm sure. He usually doesn't sleep on the bed, anyhow. Just passes out on the floor."

The salesman said that would be fine with him, if he was sure the drunk wouldn't mind. "Oh, there's one other thing," the clerk said. "Sometimes he's bad to walk around in his sleep, so we lock his door from the outside. We'll have to lock you up with him for the night."

The salesman said that was okay, he just wanted to hit the hay. Sure enough, the drunk was asleep on the floor when the clerk let him into the room, so he climbed into bed and went to sleep. In the middle of the night he awoke and needed to relieve himself in the worst way, but the bathroom was down the hall, and he was locked in, so he was up the creek without a paddle.

He got an idea. He shook the drunk, but couldn't wake him. So he pulled down the drunk's pants, squatted down a-straddle of him, and went between his legs.

The next morning he opened his eyes to see his roommate sitting up on the floor, gazing down and scratching his head. When the drunk saw he'd woke up, he said, "Buddy, are you a bad hand to drink?"

"Oh, I have one now and again," he said.

"Does it make you have to take a crap?" the drunk asked. The salesman said no, not that he'd ever noticed.

"Well, it does me," the drunk said ruefully. "At least, it did last night. Geez, I went a whole bunch. But...I'll be gol-durned if I can figure out how I missed my shorts!"

JERRY CHESNUT
Harlan, Ky.

Outhouse for Rent

(The following story was reported by a Duke University graduate, someone, it seemed to me, who was jealous of the great rivalry that has existed over the years between the University of North Carolina and North Carolina State. So it may not be true. But here it is in the Duke grad's words.—B.E.W.)

After finishing up at Duke I lived out in the country, on the family farm, and there was an outhouse on the place. I thought of tearing it down after we got indoor plumbing in the main house, but one day a UNC grad approached me, said he was looking for temporary housing. I told him I'd rent him that little brown building out there...just kidding, really, but he went out and looked it over and said it would do just fine.

So he moved in, put some carpet down, put up a TV antenna, and seemed happy as a bug in a rug. About two months later I noticed there were two TV antennas on the outhouse roof. So I asked him about it.

"Oh, I've got this friend," he said, "an NC State grad. He needed some temporary quarters, too, so I hope you don't mind, but I've sublet the basement to him!"

The Day the Outhouse Blew Up

There was this farmer who'd moved his outhouse so many times he decided it was time to build a new one; the old one was dry-rotted and in pretty bad shape. He had some dynamite left over from blasting away rock for a watering pond for his cattle. So he told everybody to stay away from the outhouse that day. Everybody did...exceptin' old Granny. She'd been in the hospital, and she had a pretty bad case of the "green-apple-quick-step," or the "barnyard trot," whichever you'd want to call it.

Granny was sitting there on the outhouse seat when the farmer touched the wires to the battery that set off that dynamite charge. Blew that outhouse sky-high, and Granny with it. She went flying through the air, landed on top of the barn, her hair all messed up and everything.

"Whoo-wee!" she said in wonder. "It's a durn good thing I didn't let that one in the house!"

He Misunderstood the Lady

One of these service station attendants was cleaning the windshield of this lady's car when she poked her head out the window and asked him, "Do you have a rest room?"

He thought she said *whisk broom,* because he'd noticed before that the floor of her car was littered with sand and paper and stuff, and he had that in mind when she asked her question.

"No, ma'am, we ain't," he said, "but if you'll back up here to the air hose, I'll blow it out for ye!"

She paid for her gas, gave him a very suspicious look, and quickly drove away.

"There ain't no understanding women!" he thought.

A Voice from Below

The mechanics and attendants at that Virginia service station were good old mountain boys, and you know how mountaineers are...they don't "take" much to people who act uppity or put on airs.

Well, they had one customer, Mrs. Snodgrass, who gave them such a hard time they hated to see her coming. "Uppity" wasn't a near good enough word to describe her high-falutin' ways. Nothing pleased her, and she always fussed about the service. "Uh, young man," she would say with a sour, put-out look on her face, "you missed a bug there on my windshield. Are you sure your gas doesn't have water in it?...My car's not running right. Tell your boss I'm coming in tomorrow to get fresh air in all my tires." She let them know she was married to the mining superintendent, just about the biggest man in the county, and she loved to throw her weight around.

One time the boys towed in a wreck that was almost totaled. The radio was smashed, too, but one of the speakers was okay, so they decided to have some fun. They put that speaker under the seat in their outhouse and hooked the wire up to their amplifier and microphone in the office. And as luck would have it, wouldn't you know the first person to come along for them to try it out on was...yep, Mrs. Snodgrass! She was serious about getting new air in her tires, the craziest thing the boys had ever heard of, but they told her it would cost two dollars per tire, for labor, if she was sure she wanted it done.

"Of course I want it done!" she bellowed. "Money is no object to me. You ought to know that. But be sure you use good, fresh air. None of that stale stuff. And while you're doing it, you might be kind enough to direct me to your, uh, powder room."

She'd never lowered herself to use their facilities before, so they figured this must be serious business. She wasn't going out there just to powder her nose. They watched her open the door and go in. About thirty seconds later, when they figured she had it in first gear and was shifting to second, they turned on the mike and spoke into it. "Uh, lady, would you mind going around to the other side. We're painting down here!"

She tore out of that outhouse like it was on fire, told them to skip the fresh air, gunned off down the road while the boys slapped their legs and bent over double laughing. They'd finally got even with Mrs. Snodgrass. And they figured she'd give a hundred dollars to know who that painter was, but, so I'm told, she's never to this day even mentioned the incident.

Expensive Toilet Paper

At a filling station near Bland, Virginia, before they got indoor plumbing, customers had to use their outhouse if they wanted to go to the bathroom.

Actually, they had two outhouses under one roof, with side doors, but they were separated in the middle only by a partition built about a foot off the floor, and running up to about six feet...similar to the rows of stalls you might find in the rest rooms in airports.

One time two men were in this outhouse at the same time. After one man finished going he noticed there wasn't any toilet paper left on the spool, but he saw the shoes of the man next door, so he pecked on the wall and said,

"Hey, bud, would you kindly share some of your paper with me? This one's empty over here."

The voice came back from the other side: "Sorry, pal, but there ain't much left over here, either. I'm afraid there's just enough for me."

A few minutes passed. There was another peck on the wall, and the first man said, "Uh, buddy...you ain't got five ones for a five, have you? Or maybe two fives for a ten?"

"I wrote some of my best sermons sitting in that old outhouse."

Rev. Randy Osborne
Berea, Ky.

5

Western Civilization and the Outhouse

Few buildings have enjoyed so many descriptive and colorful names as the privy, or outhouse. We Americans have called our outhouses by an impressive list of names:

> *the shack out back*
> *the crapper*
> *johnny or jake*
> *necessary room*
> *the throne*
> *hopper*
> *dooley*
> *biffie*
> *easer*
> *donnicker*
> *willy*
> *closet*
> *latrine*

privy
restroom
can
comfort station
head
backhouse
little house
shanty
Chic Sales
path
the sugar shack
deposit box
whatchamacallit

—as have our friends in England:

boghouse
crapping kennel
comfort station
dyke
gong house
little house
earth closet
houses of Parliament
jerry-come tumble
klondike

garden loo
nessy
nettey
place of easement
reading room
shit-hole
shittush
shooting gallery
chapel of ease
the thinking house
the throne room
slash house
the sociable
thunder box
the gun room
two seaters
the you-know-where

Many of the basic names for our outdoor conveniences derived from the Latin:

The term "privy" is an Early Middle English word which derives from the Latin *privatus,* meaning apart or secret.

"Lavatory" is French, from the Late Latin (6th century A.D.) *lavatorium.*

"Toilet," meaning washroom, is from the French "toilette," for bathing, time period unknown.

"Latrine," a place to bathe, a communal toilet, is also

French, from the Latin *latrina,* which comes from *lavatrina,* Old French, 9th to 16th century A.D.

Down through history privies existed under different conditions for common people and royalty alike. In medieval times it was monks who took the most trouble with privies, locating monasteries with drainage in mind and whenever possible building their sanitary wings close to a stream. In castles usually there was a sanitary tower with several privies to each floor, and sometimes privies were in turrets sticking out over the moats. Often they were built within chimney breasts, which kept them warm in winter, and the drafts carried away some of the smell.

The Ever-Popular Chamberpot

Toward the end of the 16th century the first real water closet was devised by Sir John Harington, Queen Elizabeth's godson, who wrote a book on the subject. But the lowly slop-jar, "thundermug," or chamberpot was by far the most popular convenience, used by one and all, as this poem, "Pisse-pots Farewell" of 1697, illustrates:

> Presumptuous pisse-pot, how did'st thou offend?
> Compelling females on their hams to bend?
> To kings and queens we humbly bend the knee,
> But queens themselves are forced to stoop to thee.

Then there is the old Scottish proverb where the thundermug speaks to us:

> Scrub me bright and keep me clean
> And I'll nae tell what a hae seen.

So our outhouses have quite a family tree, and when our forefathers crossed the ocean they brought this tradition

a 2 holer
the jennings farm
moneta, virginia
10.6.1979 bc

© boyd carr 1979

to America with them, including the practical chamberpot, sometimes affectionately called the sugar bowl. Here is an anonymous American ode called "The Passing of the Pot," not referring to a joint that is passed around and smoked, but the kind of pot that brings back memories of another day and time.

As far back in childhood as memory may go
One vessel greets me that wasn't for show.
Kept 'neath the bed where only few could see
It served the family with equal privacy.
Some called it "Peg" and some "Thundermug."
Others called it "Badger," a few called it "Jug."

Bringing it in was a chore, that's no doubt,
But heaven help the one who had to take it out!
Ours was enormous and would accommodate
A watermelon party of seven or eight.
On dark, rainy nights 'twas a useful urn.
On cold winter mornings the rim seemed to burn.

When business was rushing and extra good
Each took his turn and did the best he could.
Sometimes in a hurry, to our disgust and shame,
We fumbled in darkness and slightly missed aim.
The special one for company was decorated well
But just the same had that old familiar smell.

Today I live modern and I like it a lot
And yet I regret the passing of the pot.
For oft times I dream and it gives me a start.
How it sweetens my memory and squeezes my heart!

In Defense of a Genre

Okay, now looky, I know what you're thinking. What kind of pervert or sicko spends his life collecting outhouse stories? I mean, one or two, maybe, but isn't a whole book of this low, bathroom humor too much?

Is that what you're thinking, or am I putting words in your mouth?

And does bathroom humor have to be referred to as low?

If I were a scholar, I probably could justify this collection by pointing out that this kind of humor has served a useful purpose, at least in the Appalachian mountains where I grew up. But it would still be a defense of the material, or an apology for it. Didn't the Victorian English get their thrills reading about Lilliputians wheeling off Gulliver's giant turds in wheelbarrows, before it was acceptable even to mention anything sexual in print?

But I'm not a scholar or a folklorist. I just love stories and jokes, and I heard most of the things in this book as I was growing up in the mountains. I laughed until I almost died when I first heard some of them. I heard all kinds of stories that would be considered "folk tales," including dirty

jokes, bawdy and scatological. (Seldom did I hear them told in polite company, though, especially mixed company. It was taboo.) But I've observed, as a casual collector, that bathroom humor is the most widely acceptable in the various societies I've moved in. Many times I've started a dirty joke in mixed company only to get halfway through it and realize I was out on a limb—not knowing whether to bluff my way onward and take the embarrassment if it bombed, or to stop before the payoff and pretend I'd drawn a blank. This doesn't happen as often with bathroom jokes.

Stepping on Frogs and Barking Spiders

And there's nothing like breaking wind, on purpose or accidental, to clear the air, so to speak. At least it seems so to me, but maybe I'm just common.

For instance, once I was playing golf at the exclusive Biltmore Country Club in Asheville with my father-in-law, Dr. Arthur M. Bannerman, and a wealthy friend of his named Algie from South Carolina. We were dressed in our finest golf togs, standing on the first tee making our bets, with the stately clubhouse behind us. Sitting on a bench nearby was a very dignified-looking black man in a work shirt and overalls, probably about 75 years old, with white hair at the temples that framed an inscrutable face. Dr. Bannerman, who never met a stranger, addressed the old man and introduced us all around. It was cordial, but formal. We were reaching out to him politely and warmly, but oceans of social and cultural differences separated us. We were members. He was hired help. He nodded, hardly crinkling the lines in his proud face, but that's all he was giving. Nothing we could say or do could bridge the gap between us.

Algie addressed his ball on the tee. All was respectfully

silent as he waggled the driver. Then he farted. It broke the stately silence with a ragged crack that shocked us all...it was so out of place! He smiled, not in the least embarrassed, and shook his leg as if shaking that fart down the length of his pants, and said, "Ahhhh, that felt good!"

That inscrutable black face broke into a smile that lit up the skies over Biltmore, a warm, appreciative, understanding smile that for that moment seemed to bridge the gap between us.

Algie smiled back at him and said, "Ain't nothing like breaking wind to make a man feel good."

"Ain't it the truth!" the black man said back, laughing outright. "Ain't it the truth. It sho' is. I know what you mean." I declare, I think he would have taken us home to supper with him after that.

Outhouses as a Great Leveler of Society

So outhouse humor, with all its windy ramifications, it seems to me, often serves as a bridge between peoples of different cultures, different social groups, races and ages. It also can bridge the gap to our past, as one of the contributors to this book, Col. C.C. Albaugh, noted in a column he wrote some years ago:

> Ah, yes! Time does move on and the golden age of the outdoor privy is now over. I view its passing with mixed emotions. It was a part of life that recalls long ago, and "long ago" to me means childhood. Things seemed so simple then. I suppose that is why the rustic simplicity of the outdoor privy seems to bridge my "then" and "now." I doubt that I would return to those days even if I could, but at least my memory and recollections can bring me back for a few moments. I can be a child again. A child looking to see if the door is closed and buttoned before I start down that path to those pleasant memories of long ago.

Of course, young people of today have trouble relating to sentiment of this kind, or to the outhouse that inspired it. As Loyal Jones wrote in his book *Laughter in Appalachia* (co-written with me and put out by the publishers of this book), "I see a hesitation [by our children] and sometimes a strained laugh when the old rural jokes are told. Their experience is different from ours. A generation is a long time in the twentieth century." That is true, but I take hope in the new awareness of the environment today and in some of the back-to-the-land movements. And an awful lot of outhouse and chamberpot jokes and stories were told this past summer by young people at our Humor Festival at Berea College—told in some cases, I feel sure, by kids who had never used an outhouse. So maybe this book won't be a total air ball with young people, after all!

We live in a computer age. But I think a kid should learn how to do arithmetic before he or she learns to solve mathematical problems with a computer. Kids should learn how to spell before getting a word processor that corrects spelling for them. And I firmly believe that all kids should experience using an outhouse some time in their lives, and have to live in a house with a pump with a handle that you work up and down to coax water from the ground. I think it would help keep them in touch with the laws of supply and demand and help them better understand the sensitive balance of our earth—what you can take out and how much you can dump back in, and where.

Kids ought to know that we didn't always live in a push-button world, and that houses didn't always have flush toilets and all the water you wanted just by turning a handle. It's called "getting back to basics," and there's nothing wrong with it. That's why it's fun to leave the buttons and handles behind sometimes and go camping, rough it, get close to the earth. That's why so many people are do-it-yourselfers, why so many like to grow things, make things with their hands. It's not only educational, it's fulfilling. It makes you appreciate the comforts of home and the things you are able to buy in the store. It also helps you recognize quality and appreciate the skill and craftsmanship of others.

So...in a sense, outhouses can still be educational. And make you a better person. (Okay, I know! I'm pushing it. I'll knock it off.)

Earlier I mentioned encountering a man called Chic Sales in Jim Comstock's newspaper. Well, Charles Sale wrote a book called *The Specialist,* a very small book, maybe four by six inches, with about 20 small pages of real text. It was first published in England in 1930, had 38 "impressions," the last of which was in 1956, and sold 513,000 copies. It is a book about a man named Lem Putt (not his real name) who called himself "the champion privy builder of Sangamon County."

It is amazing to me that such a small book about

outhouses could sell that many copies! On the other hand, I was amazed that "Ode to the Little Brown Shack Out Back" sold as well as it did. It fortifies my belief that bathroom humor is the most acceptable kind of off-color humor there is. I have seen bank presidents, stockbrokers, senators, lawyers, corporation executives, ministers, teachers, and blue-collar workers laugh heartily hearing me sing my song or tell an outhouse joke.

"You forget from what humble beginnings most of the big men in this country came from," a columnist was quoted as saying in a paper published several years ago. "I'll bet my shirt that Old man John D. Rockefeller, Henry Ford, Will Rogers, Irvin Cobb and most of the older celebrities you can name, have passed many an hour in an old fashioned back-house."

But I don't think you have to have actually visited an outhouse to identify with the humor, or to find it funny. Something about the word and the image it conjures up is funny, I think.

The Fully Credentialed Outhouse Reference Book

A friend of mine, Edsel Martin, can carve a hound dog out of walnut so real-looking you can almost hear it bark. Sometimes he carves them with everything God gave them, too, such as testicles. One day a lady returned to the

Folk Art Center at Oteen, North Carolina, to buy one of Edsel's hound dogs. But she couldn't find the one she wanted, so she said to a salesperson, "I'd like to buy another of Mr. Martin's dogs." And she added shyly, "Uh...one with full credentials."

Now, I have tried to tell these tales just as I heard them, with their "full credentials." I hope the language doesn't offend you, but there just isn't any way to get around using certain words if you're going to present good, honest country humor. I mean, how can you say, "Where were you when the feces hit the fan?" Oh, you can say it, but it's not funny.

Not that certain words still don't give me a jolt when I hear them in polite company. Like the word *fart*. My mother would have washed my mouth out with soap if I had said that word in front of her growing up. I wouldn't say it in front of my mother-in-law, Mrs. Bannerman, either. But sometimes an equivalent word or phrase can be just as embarrassing, or funny—like the time my three-year-old son Travis broke wind in front of his grandmother. "Oops!" he said. "I stepped on a frog." Mrs. Bannerman laughed out loud. Encouraged by the response, Travis decided to milk it a little. He added, "Yeah, and when my daddy does it, he steps on a *bull* frog!" I blushed at this private revelation while Mrs. Bannerman laughed until tears streaked down her face. (Travis is fifteen now.)

Well, here it is, folks, all and probably more than you ever wanted to know about outhouses. It's of another day and time. But I hope you find something in it that tickles your funnybone. And I hope it makes you laugh out loud.

Billy Edd Wheeler is a playwright and songwriter whose outdoor musical drama *Young Abe Lincoln* plays each summer at Lincoln City, Indiana. His songs, including "Ode to the Little Brown Shack Out Back," "Coward of the County," "High Flyin' Bird," "Jackson," "The Coming of the Roads," and "The Reverend Mr. Black," have sold 40 million copies, as recorded by Kenny Rogers, Johnny Cash, Judy Collins, himself, and others. He is also co-author of the book *Laughter in Appalachia.* Billy Edd is available for speaking and picking-and-singing and can be reached at P.O. Box 7, Swannanoa, North Carolina 28778.